The Mystical World of Healing Crystals:
A Metaphysical Guide

Jennifer J. Barlow

Balboa Press books may be ordered through booksellers or by contacting:

Balboa Press
A Division of Hay House
1663 Liberty Drive
Bloomington, IN 47403
www.balboapress.com
1 (877) 407-4847

ISBN: 978-1-5043-5413-4 (sc)
ISBN: 978-1-5043-5414-1 (e)

Print information available on the last page.

Balboa Press rev. date: 3/31/2016

BALBOA
PRESS
A DIVISION OF HAY HOUSE

Contents

Acknowledgments

To my wonderful son; Leo James for being my muse and giving me inspiration to create this magical book and who helped to see that being myself and expressing my beliefs was perfectly ok. To my husband for showing me support and being my cheerleader. To God and my spirit guide's for also being there and giving me inspiration and sending creativity my way when I asked for help. Last, Turbo (my lost cat) for being a blessing in my life and for being my personal spiritual guardian. I will see you on the other side sweetheart.

I also would like to thank Lourdes Lebron, Tara Mideaker, and Hibiscus Moon for their support and help on my research for this book! I couldn't have done this without their help and teachings!

Introduction

I WAS CLEARING OUT MY closet one day looking for a long necklace to attach my crystal pendants to, when I open up an old jewelry box from when I was about 7, full of little pieces of Amethyst and Rose Quartz and at the bottom, a Banned Amethyst. I knew I had been attracted to Amethyst and Rose Quartz for a reason. My first two healing crystals I bought as an adult was an Amethyst and Rose Quartz. That is when I realized that I had had a personal and spiritual connection with crystals since I was just a little girl and just did not realize it! As a little girl, I would put those tiny pieces of Rose Quartz and Amethyst at my windowsill as if I thought they would appreciate the moonlight. I also felt as though the angels and God in heaven would be able to send more protection over me while sleeping. Turns out years later, these crystals love to be charged in moonlight and actually have those abilities and energies. They came into my life for a reason.

When I came to buy my first crystals as an adult, I had taught myself more and more about the healing abilities of crystals and how they could amplify intentions, candle, incense, tarot, oil, pendulum, and herbal magic. I had learned so much that I felt the need to write it down. I felt a serious connection to all this knowledge and had learned that I had known more than I realized. Then after doing a financial luck, creativity, and balance crystal grid, I had a dream that night of me reading Magical Housekeeping by Tess Whitehurst and writing down notes from her book in a notebook. When I woke the next morning, it was then that I came to realize that the crystal grid had worked. It gave me the idea through dreaming that I needed to write my own book. Why was I writing in my journal if not to share my knowledge with others to teach them in a modified way? I was only a beginner myself.

I hope *The Mystical World of Healing Crystals: A Metaphysical Guide*, will show those who are just starting, how easy and uncomplicated it is to get started and start changing your life in a positive and spiritual way.

With Love,

Jennifer J. Barlow

1

Understanding Your Chakras

Now I know you are wanting to hurry and jump into the types of crystals and what they can do for you, however it is good to know and understand your chakras first. You need to know your chakras because they are all connected to you emotionally, physically, and spiritually. When working with healing crystals, you have to know the right crystals that can help you with a particular issue or ailment. For example, if I am having horrible headaches, then I would need to know what healing crystals are associated with my brow or crown chakra (your head). I would then use a crystal associated with those chakras and after it has been fully cleansed and charged, I would focus my intention in the crystal while rubbing it or just lightly placing it on my head or forehead or in between brows.

You see how easy that was? I recognized what chakra my pain was in and easily looked up what crystals are good for that. Choose one crystal and use it. You may also use more than one if you like. Simple and easy. Now let's get started.

Here is a diagram of your chakras. The colors can help you select a crystal also. For example, the 3rd eye is in the purple color family so, I would go with an Amethyst for the crystal. Just be sure that the crystal will help with your emotional issue or ailment. If you are wondering what ailment means, it means illness or physical disorder. Either chronic or minor, does not matter. Healing crystals are able to aid in reducing pain or discomfort. Please note that they are not to replace your medications or any directions given by your doctor.

It's important to know that even though your chakras are a certain color, you do not always have to choose the matching color crystals to your chakras. For example, the 2nd chakra or sacral color is orange. However a moonstone can work on the sacral beautifully for women and men but may be more effective for women since it is a very feminine

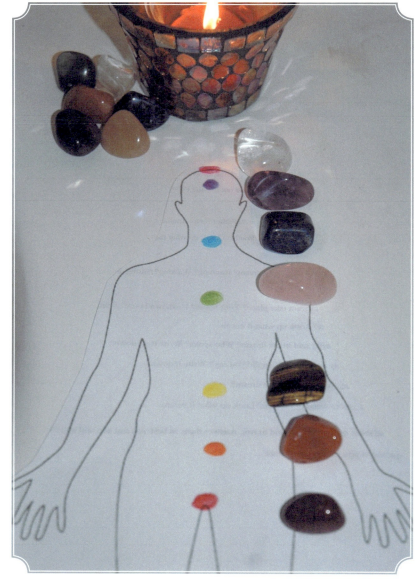

crystal because of its feminine qualities. A Moonstone is a different color but its abilities are to help the reproductive system, to conceive a baby, and the digestive system. It also helps regulate the menstrual cycle and balance hormones. So this stone would be perfect for females as it helps to embrace their goddess within. The Moonstone can also help with the 3rd eye and crown chakras. So you see how some crystals can benefit more than one chakra.

Please study this chakra chart and get to know it. It will make choosing healing crystals for those points easier. All you would have to do is pinpoint where you're aching physically, emotionally, or spiritually and then coordinate it with its correct crystal(s). Not too hard huh?

When choosing a crystal to help with a personal or emotional issue, sometimes you really do not need to find a chakra point. You can always select the healing stone or crystal that personally works for you which helps with your personal issues and just sit and meditate or pray with the crystal in your hand. Thinking and telling the crystal what you need it to do for you. Don't ever feel that you always have to match a crystal or mineral with the correct chakra and place it there. I hardly ever do unless I have physical pains. Always remember that at the end, to thank the crystal for helping you.

Please be sure that before using your crystals that you cleanse and charge them. We will get to cleansing and charging later on in the book.

List of Chakra Stones

Here are some of my personal favorite crystals that I like to use to give you an idea. These can be used for any issue you may have physically, emotional, spiritually, or personally.

Crown

Clear Quartz

Third Eye

Amethyst

Throat

Lapis Lazuli

Heart

Rose Quartz

Solar Plexus

Golden Tiger Eye

Sacral

Carnelian

Root

Red Jasper

Now that we have gotten the basics of the chakras and how you would go about choosing the crystals for them out of the way, we can get started on the types of crystals including the ones that I listed for my personal use. Please know that the way I choose my crystals is not always about what I feel I need due to some issue. I go out and buy them based on how much I am attracted to them. For example, I went to a local metaphysical store one day and was just browsing. I had a really bad headache but I didn't go there to get something for my headache, I didn't even remember I had one. I kept walking by a beautiful, rich, blue Lapis Lazuli and noticed that I was very attracted to it. I decided on getting that stone because I felt that our energies were attracted to one another. When I got home and after I took a pill for my headache, I went to look up exactly what a Lapis Lazuli could do for me online at healingcrystals.com. They have been the people I learned from about healing crystals and more specifically, I was taught by Lourdes Lebron and Tara Mideaker on the healing crystals YouTube channel. It read that a Lapis is good for the crown chakra, and is good for headaches or any pain really, as it has strong energies to help minimize pains. It is something that can be thrown in a little medicine pouch when in need of healing. I thought to myself, "This is why it wanted me to be its owner. Because it sensed that it could help me and so it drew me to it." Our energies matched and we linked together. Listening to Lourdes on the YouTube channel, I was taught that it is best to sense the energies out first and see which one speaks to you. This is how I go about choosing some of my crystals. I walk around until I am naturally drawn to one or more than one. It is something to try and experience for yourself.

List of Some Healing Crystals and Minerals

Agate

While there are many Agate stones, there are only a couple that I tend to use most; Black and Blue Lace Agate. Black Agate is associated with the root chakra and Capricorns. Black agate is a very protective and grounding stone but, has a peaceful and calmness energy as well. Helps with those who are going through loss and or mourning. Provides strength to those who need to move on and who need to find some sort of peace with a stressful or depressing situation. Put this crystal in your space or room to keep the

atmosphere calm and less stressful. It also helps to balance you emotionally. Physically it is good with problems in your joints and bones. Those who are elderly can benefit from this stone.

Blue Lace Agate is associated with the throat and third eye chakras. Also associated with Gemini and Pisces. This stone is good for activating the chakras and helps with problems in the throat. When I feel I am getting sick, I usually feel it in my head then it moves to my throat. When I feel it in my head and/or throat, I'll rub this stone on my head and throat while giving it my intention to please help reduce the discomfort. You may use it for other healing problems however. Blue Lace Agate is very calming and soothing. You or your kids can't sleep? Put this in the room to help calm your mind and body to help you fall asleep. Feel free to pair it with another soothing crystal. Do you verbally need to get something out? This crystal can help with that! It helps to express yourself in a calmly manner. It is also a very spiritual stone and helps with someone's spiritual journeys and experiences. If you feel worried or stressed,

this is the stone to go to. It is also perfect for writers to bring ideas and have the words flow out. Physically, this stone works for headaches, insomnia, and high blood pressure. Blue Lace Agate has a very "hush" energy and brings peace, balance, and lessens the stress in places. Put in your home by your front door so that only calmness and peace may enter.

Amber

Amber is very good to keep in your home. It removes negative energy and cleanses the sacred place or body. Associated with Leo, Aquarius, and Sagittarius. Also associated with the Solar Plexus. Amber would be good to hold while giving birth. Though its main chakra is the solar plexus, it can open and clean out all the chakras. Good for emotional healing such as depression. It also helps

to increase self-confidence, self-expression, and bring clarity. Amber can also help with laryngitis.

Amethyst (Said to be from the Quartz Family)

While there are many types of Amethyst, there is only one I really use and it is just simply called Amethyst. One solid color which is purple. Amethyst is associated with Pisces, Virgo, Aquarius, and Capricorn. It is also associated with the third eye and crown chakras. Amethyst is good for enhancing psychic abilities, warding off insomnia and nightmares. Physically it is good for lessening the pain of headaches and any pain on the entire head including the eyes. It absorbs negative energies, and helps to lessen the pain you feel when loosing someone. Loosing someone like in death or just a relationship, it works for that. It helps to lessen the sadness. For me, I like to combine Amethyst, Rose Quartz, and Blue Lace Agate and put it in a little tea lit candle holder and put them by my bed side so that it helps me to feel calm, relaxed, loved and provides me with loving energies. It helps me to stay asleep throughout the

night. Amethyst is a very protective crystal and encourages someone's inner self to strengthen. Like other crystals and minerals, Amethyst transforms lower vibrations into higher vibrations and then causing any negative energies to back off and allowing loving and calm energy to come forth. This is also good when wanting to connect to a high realm. I would put this on the third eye or crown chakra to enhance the ability to do so. Amethyst is good to place in the home because it is good for cleaning spaces of negative vibes and energies.

Angelite (Anhydrite)

Associated with the sign of Aquarius, the throat, crown, and third chakras. This crystal is great for wanting to connect with the high realms and helping in communication with angels or spirit guides. Because this crystal attracts angles to communicate, You can assume that this crystal is soothing, calm, peaceful, and can bring inspiration. I like to think about the crystal as my muse to help with my spiritual growth. Angelite is very similar to one of my personal favorite crystals; Selenite. Because Angelite is associated with the throat, crown, and third eye chakra, it can help in aiding those areas to be cleaned out. When someone wants to better their spiritual journey or growth and wants better communication with spiritual beings or spirit guides, then this crystal is great to use. Pair it with selenite or celestite if you are able to, and you can enhance your meditative state. You can still enhance your meditative state without pairing it though. That is just something that I would do to enhance my communication with my spirit guides twice as better.

Aventurine

Aventurine comes in many colors. The colors that I use more from my collection are the green and blue Aventurine, so we will only focus on the two but, feel free to explore more and learn about the others when you feel comfortable to do so. Green aventurine was one of my first crystals that I bought after my rose quartz and amethyst. I bought it because I associated it right off the bat with money. I then came to realize that it was great for wanting to draw in financial luck and abundance. Green aventurine is associated with the heart chakra and the signs of Virgo and Taurus. Green aventurine brings calmness, opportunity, luck, abundance, success, and is said to attract love for later in life. The crystal is also very healing and is purifying. It can increase self-confidence, leadership skills, and help to bring in creative ideas and motivation. I feel this is perfect for the office space whether in your home or at work or both. Great décor to look at, so place it on the desk to help you to remind yourself of the crystals abilities. In that way, you are still giving it the intentions you want. Physically it is good for the heart, liver, sinuses, and lungs.

Blue aventurine

This crystal is associated with the sign of Aries, the throat, third eye, and crown chakras. This crystal is great for making your senses open and making you aware of your surroundings or just the area that you are in or the people. It also helps to bring in and feel empathy, if you feel you are lacking in that area of your feelings. Sometimes I feel I should be more understanding of someone's feelings, thoughts, or beliefs. Blue aventurine is great for helping you understand a situation or person. Hold it in your hand

and ask it to help you and sit there for a minute and let it absorb your intentions. Blue aventurine can also help with addictions, selfishness, and help to bring in peace within yourself. With addictions, placing this stone on the third eye or throat chakras can help to bring in spiritual energy into those areas and help someone to understand that the addiction is coming from a deeper problem and that the addiction is a way of filling a void. This stone can help bring in spiritual development.

Aquamarine

This crystal is associated with Gemini, Pisces, and Aries. Also with the heart, thymus, and throat, and third eye chakras. This crystal is a protective stone. In fact, because it is also associated with Pisces, and Pisces element is water, it helps to protect those traveling by water. The calming and soothing energies of Aquamarine can help with fears of any kind. It is associated with the throat chakra so, it is good for verbal self- expression. It is also great for spiritual communication and helps to clear any blockages preventing you from communicating. Aquamarine is great to rise the aura and open all chakras. It is a good

companion for students as it helps to clear the mind and bring clarity. It can help to bring in more knowledge. Great for studying. Physically, aquamarine helps with problems in the throat and helps with allergies as it calms the immune system.

Black Tourmaline (Schorl)

Although there are many kinds of Tourmaline, I personally love black tourmaline. This mineral is associated with Capricorns and the root chakra. This mineral is a very protective one and great to put out side surrounding your house or just at the front and back door. Black tourmaline protects from negative energies, any psychic attacks, and anyone that wishes you harm in any way. It is said that this mineral can bring the person wishing you harm the same harm to them that they want on you. Great to wear as a bracelet or necklace or just to carry it with you. Black Tourmaline is also a great grounding stone. I also like to carry it with me to help from spending too much money when I am out shopping, because it grounds me and helps me realize "Hey! Slow down. Back away from the Michael Kors purse!" I also like to have it with me when writing because it helps me to ground myself and concentrate, and not get too distracted with other things. Even though this stone is great with protecting you and grounding you, there is also a very calming energy to it. It helps me to keep

calm when in traffic, especially when I am angry at those crazy drivers on the road. I just grab it and hold it. Place this mineral in your home to create a calming atmosphere and protect that room or space from negative entities. Black tourmaline protects all chakras although its main chakra is said to be associated with is the root. It boosts people's self-esteem and helps in lessening worry. Physically, black tourmaline helps to boost and strengthen someone's immune system, balance the hemispheres of the brain, and helps with problems with the lungs. I always feel that I can think clearly when my black tourmaline is with me and I feel very balanced and in control which is not like me to be honest. I am a very scattered brain person when trying to think right away or have to figure out something quickly. My mind tends to wonder off and not focus. This mineral helps me to be on point.

Black Onyx

Black Onyx is associated with Leo, Capricorn, and the root chakra. Black Onyx is another very protective stone. It protects against negative energies and those who wish you harm. I carry black onyx when I travel whether it be far or near so as to protect me from any danger. It can also help with providing strength in time of fear. When waking up from a bad dream, I hold black onyx in my hand as I pray to my God and ask that he and the mineral give me strength to get over the fear that has come over me. Black onyx can give strength in times of weakness as well. The times that you feel

you need strength, this mineral is great to carry with you. Black onyx also provides encouragement. If you are nervous about a job interview for example, then carry this stone with you to give you strength and courage to get you through the interview. This mineral is good for getting through stress, sadness, and grief. It can also bring happiness and good fortune. Physically, it is good for aiding in the recovery of addictions, good for getting over allergies, aids in childbirth, and helps with any problems in the legs.

Bloodstone

Bloodstone is associated with Aries, Libra, Pisces, the root, sacral, solar plexus, and heart chakras. Bloodstone is good to purify and detox the body. It cleanses the body and grounds negative energies. Although this crystal may not look like it can help with love, don't let the appearance trick you, it is good for bringing in love into any situation. When I am in a difficult argument and it effects my moods, I carry bloodstone to help bring love into the situation and help me switch my feelings and thoughts from negative to positive. It can also help clarify situations as if the light bulb switched on in your head and you say "oh I get what that means now!" Bloodstone can also be used for increasing strength and energy.

It can remove the energy blockages that someone may have and help them create calm energy flow. Bloodstone is good to take with you if you are looking to enhance your creativity and intuition. Physically, it is good with fatigue, confusion, to cleanse energy, purifying blood and detoxes the spleen, liver, and kidneys. It can regulate the blood flow, and cleanse the lower chakras.

Carnelian

Carnelian is associated with Cancer, Leo, and the sacral chakra. Carnelian is great for enhancing creativity. I place it near me when I am in need of some creative ideas whether it would be for a book or college classes. It helped to bring in ideas and provided focus so that I may get my work done. It is also a great crystal to help with acceptance, particularly acceptance of life. It can increase power within one's self, physical energy, and courage. Because it can help to focus, this crystal is great for meditating and helping with concentration. If you find yourself getting very angry, carry carnelian to help calm the anger. Physically, it can help with PMS, problems with the bladder, liver, spleen, and kidney, and increases blood circulation.

Citrine

Citrine is associated with Gemini, Aries, Libra, Leo, the sacral, solar plexus, and crown chakras. It also cleanses all chakras. I like to use citrine in my abundance or financial luck grids because its energies and vibrations are able to provide that for you. Citrine has a very uplifting and joyful vibration that spreads out to you and others around you. It helps you see the positive side of things. This makes it good for you when you are in a stressful or depressed situation. It helps to overcome depression, stress, and anger. It is also good for bringing in ideas and creativity and also attracting success. When I do my financial luck grids, I also use citrine to help with finding success and having balance in my life. This crystal is great to carry with you or just keep in office spaces and the home so that it can continue to balance your life and help attract that success. Citrine is also good for warding off negativity which makes it a protective crystal. Pair it with black tourmaline or onyx and you have your protective shield up. Great to wear as a piece of jewelry. Physically, citrine is good for problems with the spine, digestive organs, metabolism, aiding in detoxifying the body. It also helps with circulation. Because it loves to be charged by the energizing and warm sun, it is also good for giving energy.

Emerald

This is a crystal that I am very attracted to and I personally love. Emeralds are associated with the heart chakra, Taurus, Gemini, and Aries. I have felt the loving energies of emeralds and I love it. It not only helps me feel love but it brings love to me and sends it out. If you are looking for love, then wearing emerald will help draw in and bring love to you. Very strong in the love department. Not only is it good for love but also for bringing wisdom, loyalty, bonding and unity. Perfect for a love grid! Emeralds are also great for bringing in hope in negative situations and sending hopeful vibes and thoughts to others.

It can help with understanding and strengthen communication. This crystal can also increase memory and clarity. When meditating with emerald, it can help to open your heart chakra and help with feeling blessed with what you have in life. Owning emerald can help you to follow your heart and provides courage. This stone can also make a great healing crystal as it aids and supports in the recovery of any illness or chronic condition.

Fluorite

Fluorite comes in a few colors and all have similar but different abilities. I happen to have all colors except yellow and rainbow. So let's get to the colors that I have. Feel free to look up rainbow or yellow fluorite at healingcrystals.com. This site I recommend when you are just a beginner.

Blue Fluorite is associated with Pisces, Capricorns, the throat, and third eye chakras. Blue Fluorite is great for having clear communication whether it be on a spiritual plane or when communicating with people. This crystal brings in energies of peace and helps to bring inner peace. It is good to carry with you when you are around people who tend to speak their mind not considering others around them and not knowing their limit of when to not talk. This crystal can help to calm your actions and words towards those kinds of personalities. Put blue fluorite in your home to protect from arguments and "butting heads". Physically, blue fluorite helps with illnesses of the ears and throat, inflammation, and Alzheimer's. Also helps to improve the immune system, and can help people who have had brain trauma as it improves speech.

Green Fluorite

This crystal is associated with Pisces, the heart, and throat chakras. Green Fluorite can help when you are not feeling upbeat or like you have no energy. It helps to energize you. It is also a great cleanser as it has strong energies to help to do so. It helps to energize all chakras. Green fluorite is great for healing the heart physically and emotionally. Increases intuition and helps calm overactive energies or situations. This crystal is also good for keeping away any negativity, it increases concentration, and keeps someone focused. Excellent for work and school. I love to have my fluorite's with me when working because I get so much done, I'm focused, and it encourages me to achieve my goals for the day and get everything organized. Green fluorite can also bring insight into someone's life and inner growth. If you are looking to connect with nature spirits, green fluorite can help with that, specifically water. Put green fluorite in your garden to attract hummingbirds and butterflies. Physically, it can boost the immune system and cell regeneration. It can help calm arthritis pains, heal scars physically and emotionally, sore throats, insomnia, upset stomach, and ulcers.

Purple Fluorite

Associated with Pisces, Capricorn, the crown, and third eye chakras. Same as the blue and green fluorite, it helps increase intuition, creativity, and focus. It also helps with thinking quickly, aids with bone marrow illnesses, and helps those with learning disabilities. I love to have this around to help me with my creativity, shoot out ideas, and if I have writers block.

Garnet

I love garnet. There are a few different kinds but the one I have and will talk about is the red garnet. Garnet is associated with Leo, Virgo, Capricorn, Aquarius, the root, sacral, and heart chakras. This stone is about love, loyalty, and commitment. Perfect for a love grid whether you are looking for love or looking to enhance your relationship that you are in now. Garnet helps to deal with depression, gives and draws in joy, provides hope to those seeking it, and helps to lessen anger. This stone also helps to increase will power and courage to any situation. Garnet helps to release feelings that you may have towards someone and allows you to express those

feelings. Garnet cleanses and re-energizes the chakras associated with it. It balances sex drive and the sacral chakra. It also brings and sends out energies of passion, love, loyalty, devotion, and commitment. Like I said, it is perfect for a love grid whether you are asking to attract someone of a particular astrological sign, attract loving energies from your surroundings, or want to send loving energies to someone or place.

Hematite

Associated with Aries, Aquarius, and the root chakra. It is a very detoxifying, balancing, and grounding stone. I carry hematite to help ground myself while I go shopping so that I do not over spend. If I do not already have a grounding stone by me, I keep Hematite by me when I do work because it keeps me from wondering off in thought or helps to prevent me from distraction. I really get work done when I have this stone with me. Hematite is also good for keeping negative energy from you and sucks in the negative energy before it reaches you. This is a stone that you have to cleanse a lot because of this! Hematite also helps you see the greater and more positive side of negative situations. It is great for cooperation. Great when around someone you tend to butt heads with a lot. It will help you to cooperate with them. If you feel that you are not sure what it is you are good at, holding hematite and asking it to show you what you are good at, is great! This stone helps you to find that out. I have inner ear issues so my

balance can be off at times. Hematite can help with balancing the equilibrium. Physically, hematite can protect against electromagnetic smog and is great for the blood and liver. It is highly detoxifying. Remember to cleanse it often!

Jasper

There are lots of types of jasper but, the 3 types I have are brecciated, red, and zebra jasper. Although these kind are associated with different signs and chakras, all jaspers are known as the ultimate nurturers. It helps to support those in difficult times and stress. Jasper is used in Shamanic journeying and helps with dream recall and facilitates them. Jasper is a protective stone, and like most minerals and crystals, helps to absorbs negative energies. Jasper can also bring someone courage when needed and also determination. When in need to focus whether with work, school, or just working out, and need that boost of focus and motivation, Jasper can help with that. I take Jasper with me to the gym sometimes and it helps to keep me moving. Jasper is also great to stimulate creativity. Awesome for when you feel stuck in a situation or work as it brings some ideas and helps expand your imagination. Business people can benefit from jasper. Try pairing it with green aventurine and leave it in the office or home office. Physically, it helps those in times of emotional help like those going through addictions and abuse. Jasper helps with problems in the legs, nausea,

intestines, pancreas, and urinary-tract. Also helps to ward off nightmares. With the 3 different ones I have, brecciated is associated with Aries, Scorpio, the root, and solar plexus chakras. Brings focus vitality, and is a very grounding stone. The red jasper is associated with Aries, Scorpio, the root, and sacral chakras. It is a very nurturing stone like all Jaspers, and is very stabilizing. Last is the zebra jasper, it is a very comforting stone and can help to center you and ground you. This Jasper is associated with Leo, Scorpio, and the root chakra.

Labradorite

Labradorite is one that I tend to gravitate towards no matter what. If I am not sure of what crystal to take with me, I always just grab my labradorite. I have a certain relationship and attraction with this crystal. It helps to cleanse and open all your chakras and your entire aura. It also protects them!

Labradorite is associated with Sagittarius, Scorpio, Leo, the third eye, and the crown chakra. This crystal is very mystical as it increases intuition and increases psychic abilities, so try using this on your crown and third eye! This crystal is great for balancing your intuition and intellect. It is a good crystal to help bring out true intentions. It can strengthen your auras and prevent energy leaks. When you are going through some kind of transformation or change, carry labradorite with you so that it can help to ease you into that

change and not have it overwhelm you. The crystal can help someone to see their inner worth, heal any past life issues and just any past memory, and can help prepare you for ascension. It can also help when communicating with someone's high self. Labradorite is also an amplifier, so put this near or in your grids to amplify your intentions and energies placed on the grid. Physically, it is good for any pains in the stomach, warts, and problems with eyes, the brain, addictions, and it increases metabolism. This is a crystal that everyone should own!

Lapis Lazuli

I love this stone. I walked into a crystal store and my attention at that time went straight to Lapis, just like I had mentioned in the beginning of the book. So, it is safe to say that Lapis Lazuli is great for head pains. Lapis Lazuli is associated with Sagittarius, Libra, and the throat, third eye, and crown chakra. I love carrying this stone with me because it helps me to see my inner power, increase my intuition, and enhance my communication with people. With communicating with others, it helps to verbally express yourself truthfully and makes it easier to calmly express your reason for anger. Lapis is great for not only opening the throat chakra but also the third eye as it helps to connect with physical and celestial kingdoms. It helps those to feel peaceful and bring wisdom when entering mystical realms

and communicating with spirit guides. This stone holds the ability to spiritual attainment. This powerful and mystical stone also protects one from psychic attacks, guards from negative energies which, what happens after that is, that energy bounces back to its original sender or location. Remember, what you give out is what you attract! Great to wear or carry while out and about. Physically, Lapis can help with the thyroid, nervous, and immune system. It is great for reducing headache or migraine pain, and fevers.

Larimar

I love this stone and have always been attracted to larimar because of how comforting it makes me feel when holding it. Larimar (also known as Pectolite) is associated with Leo, Pisces, and the throat, third eye, and crown chakras. It is a very high vibrational, and nurturing stone. Larimar can come in other colors such as white, green - blue, or deep blue. This stone helps to provide clear communication, clarity, the truth, calmness, and balance to a situation. It also helps to remove stress and negativity. When going through some kind of change, it helps someone to move through the change smoothly. It is said to have a strong connection to the sea and dolphins. Perhaps the reason why I am attracted to this stone is because my sign is Pisces and my element is water. Because larimar is very nurturing, it helps to heal the body, soul, and mind. It is great with helping to get to a deep meditative state and connection

with spirit guides, other angles, source, and guardians. Physically, larimar is great at aiding in the healing process of chemical imbalances, infections, and mood disorders.

Moonstone

Moonstone is one of my favorite stones in my collection. Every time I am wearing it or carrying it, it brings out the best of me. It helps me to feel comfortable in my own skin. Moonstone is associated with Cancer, Libra, Scorpio, and the sacral, third eye, and crown chakra. It increases intuition, brings inspiration, and Goddess like energy. The reason why it helps me to feel good in my own skin is because of the Goddess energies it provides specifically to females. It helps us females to embrace who we are and the Goddess within us, although this stone can also help with males as well. It helps to balance the emotions and any aggressive tendencies. Moonstone helps to relieve stress because of its soothing energies it releases. It is said to protect those that travel on or by water. Moonstone sends the divine inspiration to our intuition. It also helps with decision making, making it easier. When in need of creativity, the moonstone can provide that and also with bringing patience. Physically, this stone can help with conception by helping with the reproductive system. It can also help with balancing hormones and the menstrual

cycle. Moonstone is good for regulating sleep patterns and warding off nightmares, perfect to place in a safe place within a child's bedroom!

Obsidian

There are different types of obsidian but, the one's I tend to use are the rainbow and black obsidian stones. It is associated with the sign; Cancer and the root chakra. Rainbow and black obsidian are very grounding and protective stones. They have the ability to provide happy energies. When around these stones, I tend to get very silly! They just boost my happiness. Because of their happy energy, it can turn a bad day into a good day and rid of bad luck. Not only can they provide happy energies but it can also help to rid of fears that are overwhelming or hard to overcome. Because obsidain is very protective and grounding, it helps to cleanse someone of negativity and emotions such as, envy, anger, greed, resentment, and other emotions. They also help to bring truths out and in the open. Perfect to hold with you when in conversation with friends and family.

Peridot

This crystal is associated with Virgo, Leo, Scorpio, Sagittarius, and the heart, and solar plexus chakras. It is a good healing crystal as well as a protective and comforting crystal. Peridot is good for aiding those who are going through traumatic and emotional experiences. It helps to bring out and feel unconditional love, and helps to reduce the effects of the ego. Peridot can also help in understanding the types of relationships people have in their lives and what they mean to that person. It can be romantic, a friendship, family, or just people at work. This crystal can also balance and align the chakras. This is good to do after undergoing any energy healing of the body. Physically, it is said to be good at assisting in childbirth. It is also good for aiding in healing the heart, lungs, and stomach.

Quartz (Clear, Rose, and Smokey)

There are many types of Quartz. I love the Quartz family! The ones that I have and are going to discuss are the clear, rose, and smokey quartz. The clear quartz to me is the ultimate crystal to use in order to amplify all energies. This crystal is said to work with just about everything. Therefore, this quartz is associated with all the astrological signs and chakras. I tend to use this crystal in all my crystal grids as it amplifies my intentions. This crystal is said to be known as the power stone as it is the most powerful of the mineral kingdom. If you are starting out and not sure where to begin when it comes to buying your first crystal, you should choose the clear quartz. I have it in

my grids, in my house in just about every room, and outside by my front door and in my plants. I have a lot! I gave them the intentions that anyone who comes to my house will leave their negativity outside. The clear quartz is used as an invisible shield at my door. Imagine someone entering my home and seeing their negativity left outside as they came in with their positive energies. It stays outside. So, this crystal is used for all kinds of healing. Because it absorbs so much, it is best to cleanse this crystal often.

Rose quartz is another one of my favorites. I love it because it helps me to feel loving energies from others and helps to express my love to others. Rose helps with all types of love, it brings compassion, and self-esteem. Rose quartz is associated with Taurus, Libra, and the heart chakra. So it makes sense that this crystal helps to open the heart to feel all types of loving energies. Rose has a very calming and soothing vibe to it. When you feel tension between you and another, or between people, or in your space, rose is great to hold to help bring in the love into the room and bring in the calming vibes to lower down the tension. If you have negative emotions going through you for a reason you may know, holding this crystal to your heart chakra and relaxing, it will

releasing the negative energies from you. It absorbs the energy to help heal you. Rose quartz can also help in healing a broken heart. Great for a "healing the heart" kind of grid. Physically, it is good for aiding in the healing of heart issues,

breast cancer (good supporting crystal), vertigo, asthma, and sexual issues. It can also balances sex drive, and helps with face complexion. This is why make-up contains bits of rose quartz minerals!

Now let's move on to smokey quartz. Smokey quartz is associated with Capricorn, Scorpio, and Sagittarius. It is also associated with the root and solar plexus chakras. This stone is a great healer as it absorbs and wards off negative energies and entities. It is also great for clearing the auric field and protecting the aura as well. It provides psychic protection and helps to keep you grounded. It also protects against electromagnetic pollution. Place this stone under your pillow at night, and it will help to enhance your dreams state. Physically, smokey quartz helps in aiding the healing process for cancer, chemotherapy, radiation, headaches, abdomen, tumors, and the legs. It is also good at balancing out the body.

Rhodonite

Associated with Taurus, the heart, and root chakra. This crystal brings self-love and sends love to others. It is also a very supportive crystal for those who have breast cancer. My step mom had breast cancer and I did distant healing for her using this crystal. She too has this crystal with her. So, it is great for that. Rhodonite is also good for attracting love and keeping negative energies away. This crystal is good for reminding someone to spread love and to help others out sometimes. This crystal can also help to reveal what someone's true passion is and gives them a boost of motivation to pursue that passion. Physically, this stone is known for helping with problems in the liver and organs. Also, ailments in the nervous system, lungs, and heart.

Selenite

I love this mineral! Selenite is such a calming, soothing, and peaceful mineral! In fact, I place selenite, blue lace agate, rose quartz, and amethyst by my bed side to help me feel relaxed, calm, and like I am ready to just pass out and sleep. Selenite is associate with Taurus, the crown, and higher crown. This delegate mineral has a very high vibration, and is great to help reach Christ consciousness, and communicate with spiritual beings. This is such an angelic mineral. Selenite can grant you protection given from the angelic realm and can help to completely vanquish negative energies. Place selenite in each room or surrounding your home outside to create a peaceful and safe place. This mineral can also bring clarity to a situation and also bring mental clarity. Someone can enter their past or future lives with this mineral. Great for activating the chakras it is associated with but, you may find that it is great for activating other chakra points as well, and that is just fine. Each mineral and crystal works differently with different people. Selenite can also help with making your memory stronger. If you have selenite, you would notice that it kind of reminds you of fragile bones, this is interesting because physically, it is good for working with the skeletal system and spine.

Sodalite

Sodalite is associated with Sagittarius, the throat, and third eye chakra. This stone increases your intuition, focuses energy, and brings guidance to situations. This is great for getting into a deep meditative state. It also helps with those who may be over-emotional, as it brings balance to their emotions. Sodalite enhances psychic abilities, and helps to trust in your own judgment. This stone can bring discipline in someone's life and can help to find a career path and advancement. Holding sodalite or wearing it throughout the day can bring different ways of dealing with problems and tasks. It can also help someone in realizing the patters they make in their life whether it be a positive or negative pattern, it helps to bring that to your attention. Physically, sodalite can help someone to relax and calm down if they feel nervous or anxiety. It also helps with phobias and or fears, confusion, and panic attacks. This stone can also strengthen the immune system.

Tiger Eye

There are about 4 types of Tiger Eye crystals. The one I have is the one that most people know of, and that's the golden tiger eye. I love this crystal. I feel so protected when I'm around it, holding it, or wearing it. It was one of the first crystals that I owned but was unaware of its abilities, when I was around 7 years old. When I was older, I found out that the crystal was supposed to be a very protective crystal, this is because I had seen a movie with Sandra Bullock and Nichole Kidman called "Practical Magic". I loved that movie.

This Tiger eye crystal is associated with the signs of Leo and Capricorn, and the sacral, solar plexus, and third eye chakra. Tiger Eye is great for bringing protection from negative energies, anything that anyone wishes bad on you, an unsafe area, etc. It protects against just about anything however, it is like being invisible but that is not to say that nothing at all could happen to you, it is just less likely. Tiger eye can also bring creativity and balance. It can also help with bringing insight into a problem. Tiger Eye brings good luck, prosperity, and protects against curses and bad luck. Use this as a talisman in your

home. Tiger eye is also great for aiding in manifestation rituals and helping to form them into reality. This crystal helps bring courage through times of change. You can use this crystal to help build your inner personal power. It can balance the lower chakras, increase psychic abilities, motivation, control, concentration and focus. Physically, it is good for those who go through depression and or bipolar disorder, having problems with the eyes, fatigue, and issues in the throat. Great to have in your medicine bag.

Now that I listed some stones for you and how they can help you, I want to move on to the next chapter. The second chapter I find very interesting and I hope you will too. It is very important to know exactly how the healing stones and crystals work on the scientific level so, let's move on!

The Science behind Crystal Healing

EVERYTHING AND EVERYONE ARE IN fact connected energetically and to each other. We all share vibrations. This is something that the Ancient's like the Egyptians, Shamans, and Native American Indians tried and still try to explain to us through their teachings today, and through their ancient texts. A way that I can explain it is like this: we are all influenced energetically from everything and everyone. We are influenced by our emotions and other's emotions, and a part of that is because of our non-crystalline structure. Non-crystalline means that we are not formed the way that crystals and minerals are formed. We do not have the same characteristics as crystals. Our bodies give and receive vibrations very easily. The vibrations "can move out of its dominant oscillatory rate (DOR) so very easily when we experience any type of stress. We are also made of many varying oscillatory rates as our organs and even cells have all their own DORs. " (Moon, 2015). It is because of our DORs that almost anything can intrude our energy field and cause a reaction. Because of the crystals perfect geometric structure, their DORs are very balanced. So when we work with crystals and minerals, we are relying on their balanced vibrational frequencies which effects ours because we absorb it. "The abilities to heal and vibrate at the correct frequencies are already present within the cells of any living being's body, just waiting to oscillate with the correct frequencies." (Moon, 2015).

Our body is made up of 9 systems, which are the urinary, skeletal, respiratory, reproductive, nervous, muscular, endocrine, digestive, and the circulatory. They each have different dominant oscillatory rates (DORs). All the cells within each of the systems are made up of atoms. They are made up of subatomic particles. The particles break down and dissolve creating vibrations of tightly pressed energy.

So this chapter was just a quick lesson on the science behind the vibrations and energies of crystals and minerals and how they work. It is important to know this information because I feel that when working with these crystals, we have to know everything such as their names, abilities and how they operate, and also so that we can teach others who may not understand how they work! Most people do not know that there is a science backing up the energies and vibrations that we feel from these amazing crystals and minerals but, there is and it is important to spread the word!

Cleansing and Charging Your Crystals

THIS CHAPTER IS ANOTHER VERY important chapter as it relates to the care of yourself and your crystals and minerals. Cleansing your crystals and mineral are important because of the energies that surround both you and your crystals, and the energies that you both have given off and absorbed. Everyone is different and can feel energies and vibrations differently. Some may feel sick because of the many energies that one crystal holds while others are not as effected by the energies. Cleansing your crystals can help to release all those energies that were absorbed into the crystal, making it open now, to your own individual positive energy. It is good to always cleanse your crystals whether they are out in different places in your house, or you are wearing them as jewelry or just in your pocket, or even kept in containers. You have to cleanse every once in a while, every day if you are wearing them or are keeping them in your pocket or bag. The more energies and negative energies it collects, the more it is going to bring down your own energies and drain you. You want to be filed with positivity so, cleanse, cleanse, cleanse!

Charging your crystals and minerals is just as important as cleansing because this is how you are able to amplify those intentions that you set on your crystals. You are charging the crystals to work to their fullest potential for you!

There are a few ways of cleansing your crystals and minerals. The first way I would like to share with you is by water and fire. Water is a great way of cleansing your crystals as it washes away any negative and unwanted energies. All you would have to do is grab your crystal or crystals and run them under cool water. Never too cold or too hot. You want it to be about room temperature. As you

are washing them, state what it is you are wanting to cleanse from the crystals. For example, "I cleanse you all of any negative and unwanted energies and any energies that are not of my own." Repeat that about 3 times and mean it! Once you are done, dry them off on a towel and you are good to go with charging them. Please note that no mineral such as Celestite, Pyrite, Kyanite, or Selenite should touch water. Ever! These are minerals that and are too delicate to be washed in water. I will talk about another way of cleansing those minerals later on in the book.

Fire is another way of cleansing your crystals and minerals. The hot energies generating from the flame is cleansing and warding off all the negative energies. Never place a crystal or mineral directly

in fire. Simply light a medium to small candle within its candle holder and place the crystals and minerals around the candle like shown above.

Incense and smudging is another great way of cleansing. Please note that if you buy incense and you notice some oils wiping off on the incense packaging, then those incense are not safe to use around your crystals and minerals as the oils from the incense can damage your crystals and minerals. Please be sure to check the packaging before buying. If no oil is rubbing off then it is safe to buy. Try buying Nag Champa, Sandalwood, or Frankincense to do the cleansing! The incense smoke which used in other ancient cultures and even medieval times, were used to ward off any unwanted and negative energies. If you go to church and see the priest waving incense, it is almost always either Sandalwood or Frankincense. They are cleansing the environment and the people. So cleansing your crystals and minerals is the same! Simply light your incense stick or your sage stick, put in an incense holder or safe container to burn in, and hold your crystals or minerals over where the smoke is and cleanse away! Again you want to state what you want the crystals or minerals to be cleansed of. Please never leave your incense or sage burning if you are not there to watch it!

Smudging works the same only the smoke is much thicker so if you have sprinklers in your home that can go off, I do not recommend smudging inside. Try doing outside instead! Perhaps in your magical sacred garden!

When smudging, you want to light the smudge stick, wait till it really lights and smokes, then, blow the flame out. Once you blow out the flame, the smoke will start to come and you are able to now smudge and cleanse your crystals and minerals! Try using sage sticks or palo santo! Please never leave them on. Once you are finished cleansing, you have to burn out the stick!! Do not leave it going!

The other types of cleansing is super simple! No fire or water! Instead you can use potting soil or just dirt from outside! What is great about this method is that you are using nature that the crystals and minerals call home and are used to; earth! This cleanses them super well! When I do this, I like to leave them in the soil or dirt for about 2-3 days so that they not only cleanse but, they get a sense of "being home". The dirt or soil cleanses the crystals of all the energies absorbed within it. It releases it! When you pick up the crystal or mineral after it is done cleansing, you really feel the difference! You feel that the vibrations come off the crystal or mineral is different and you feel the relief! See how simple that method is! I have crystals in my

plants outside and inside because I know that they appreciate it and in return, I get great and positive results! You may also place them in sand. Please note that, the soil and sand must be dry! You do not want to put delicate minerals in wet soil!

Charging

The first method of charging that I would like to talk about is the lunar energy of the moonlight! Moonlight generates great, soothing, yet strong energies. Its energies are very intuitive, slow, calming, connects you to different realms, and dreams. So it is a great time to try and connect with your spirit guides and angles. I always feel drawn to placing my crystals under moonlight as I feel that it charges best, especially under a full moon! The lunar energies from a full moon are amplified! Your crystal will be ready to work and give all they got to help manifest what it is you feel you need! So keep those astrological and lunar calendars close by so that you know exactly when there is a full moon, blue moon, or super moon!

The second method is by sun light! Sun light I feel is fun energy and very, very energetic energy. It brings in motivation and joy! I always feel drawn to charging my citirine, amber, carnelian, tiger eye, smokey quartz and clear quartz crystals under the sun light. These crystals anyway, provide me with motivation, energetic, and happy energies! So

to amplify those energies by charging them with the energies and rays of the sun, really give me an energy boost! Great to take with you in the mornings to work instead of grabbing that soda or coffee to wake you up!

Simply place your crystals either outside or at the window where the sun can hit them. Please be careful and pay attention to how hot that spot is from the sun at your window. If it is way too hot, take them to a place where there is shade and not so hot but where some sun light can still hit them. Best to put them in plants outside or in your garden where they have enough shade and do not get too hot! Crystals can be great for the life of your garden anyway! Allowing the sun light to bring them amplified energies, which can amplify your intentions toward those crystals and help to manifest more, what it is you need from them.

Another method of charging is by candle light! Simply place your crystals around a candle and you are all done! The energies generating off of the flame will help to charge your crystals! Make sure that your candle is in a candle container or glass so that the candle itself is not touching the crystals. You do not want the wax to fall on your crystals and ruin them.

The last method is by using large crystal clusters or just large crystals! I recommend the clear quartz crystal, as it is known as the "ultimate cleanser and amplifier". You are able to place other crystals on them and they will charge that way as well. Just make sure that the large crystal is cleansed and charged the way you feel it should be in order to charge other small crystals. I first learned this watching Lourdes and Tara on their healing crystals YouTube Channel.

Another way is by putting your smaller crystals in a crystal tea light candle holder. I have a rose quartz tea light candle holder. I love putting my other smaller crystals in the hole where the tea light candle goes, because the crystals are totally engulfed in the larger crystal and are able to charge with the loving energies that the large rose quartz provides.

Creating Crystal Grids

CRYSTAL GRIDS ARE VERY POWERFUL ways of getting something that you want to manifest, manifest. Please note that you should never wish anything bad upon anyone. You should always wish the best for people. Crystal grids are for you and you only and always make sure that you are doing these grids out of the love and kindness of your heart. Moving on, crystal grids are used to help us with many things and situations in life. It can be anything from finding and attracting love, to helping you have a better night sleep. You can set up crystal grids anyway you like. It all needs to come from within. If you feel you need to only use pyramid crystals in your grid, then do it. If you feel you need to only use small tumbled stones in your grid, then do it. It all has to come from within and what feels right. With me, I always need to use my clear quartz crystal points in my grids. They never let me down. With grids you have to make sure to cleanse and charge your stones and crystals before going forth to using the grid. You then have to set your intention to the grid and focus on what you feel you need in your life. Last, you then have to activate it.

To begin, pin point what you feel you need in your life. Is it finding a job? Is it finding a best friend? Find out what you feel you need, then pick out the stones, crystals, and minerals that you feel can do the job for you and manifest what you want. For me, when I do my financial luck and abundance grid, I always feel that Citrines, Green Aventurine, Green Quartz, Carnelian's, Red Jasper's, Hematite's, and of course my Clear Quartz cluster or points work best. So I have those in my grid. You choose what you know can do the job for you and always make sure to thank your crystals for helping you.

When setting up your grid, you have to be sure that the center crystal or mineral set the overall intention. For example, when wanting to attract love, your overall intention is love and attracting, so rose quartz can help with that or an emerald. I recommend you start off at this point, with putting one or those in the center of the grid. The center stone also represents you, so when setting your intention, hold that stone in your hand for a moment or two, focusing on what you want. I prefer to meditate with it and focus on what I want and see myself accomplishing my goal and receiving what I need. Then I put it in the center. The center point is everything. Please make sure you are choosing your center crystal wisely. It sometimes helps me to write on a piece of paper my intention and slip it either on top or under the center crystal. This can help personalize and amplify your intention.

When setting up the rest of your grid please make sure that your crystals are already cleansed and charged. The rest of the crystals are kind of like your messengers. They help you to receive what it is you feel you need, so using the same example on attracting love, I would use rose quartz hearts all around my grid, only about 4 but if you wish for more or less, that is ok. It all depends on you and how you feel about it. Rose quartz is what is going to find the love and attract it to you. Of course, you may use any other crystal or stone to place around your grid. I am only giving an example. Another crystal to use would be citrine, because it helps to attract what you want, not just love. It helps to enhance the success of the intention. The rest are crystals that represent what you want in that relationship. Is it commitment?

Loyalty? Good communication? Try garnet for commitment and loyalty and either blue kyanite or sodalite for good and calm communication. Then you would put those around your center crystal as well.

Once you have found all your crystals and minerals that you want, you then have to activate your grid. There are different ways to do this. You can just use your hand, wand, or pendulum to do this. I prefer to use my crystal wands for this. It can be any wand you like. I like to use my selenite wand because using selenite, I see it as asking your guides for assistance in getting what you need from your grid and what you want to manifest. So you simply take your wand, hand, or pendulum and wave it over your grid however you like. It can be in a waving motion, it can be in a circular motion which I do, or it can outline the grid almost making the motion of creating the flower peddles of a flower, moving in then out and out lining the crystals. Those are ways of activating your grid. When doing so, make sure to state in your head or out loud what you would like the grid to do for you. If you are trying to attract love, you could say something like "I activate you to help me attract love and find someone who will be loyal, committed, be my best friend, love me for who I am, and provide affection and passion into our relationship. Thank you." Then you are done. You can add to that if you like or just say something else. Does not matter because it depends on how you feel it should go. Please remember to always thank the crystals when you are done.

When activating your grid, try to imagine white light beaming from your hand, wand, or pendulum. You can imagine the white light doing whatever comes to mind when activating your grid. I like to imagine my white light shooting from my hand or wand and throughout all my crystals and then shooting up to the sky and filling the earths skies as if it is searching to help find what I am looking for and bringing it to me.

When everything is set up and done, try to remember to cleanse and charge your grid at least once every week. It is drawing in and picking up energies from the outside world whenever you walk by it or others do. I just leave my grid the way it is and wave Frankincense above it until it coats my grid in smoke. Then to charge, I sometimes put the grid on a plate of some sort and leave it in the sun for no more than 15 minutes or in the moonlight overnight.

Have fun with this and remember that we must never wish anything bad on anyone. Always do grids for yourself or to heal someone of a sickness or pain, and always use the grids with good intentions, love, and angelic light.

5

Plants / Herbs

ANOTHER THING THAT OUR ANCESTORS did and are still practiced today is herbal magic. You can look at it as magic or you can look at it like they have their own vibrations and energies. Everything that comes from the earth, has energy and vibrations that interact with our own vibrations and energies. If you want to attract love, try wearing a strand of maidenhair fern and pink rose pedals. If you want to bring in some financial luck, you can burn whole cloves as incense, or if you want to boost your psychic abilities, burn acacia with sandlewood. There are so many things that herbs can do to help us just like crystals and minerals can. You just have to make sure you know what the plants and herbs do. I will give you a short list of herbs and tell you what ways you can use them and what crystals can coexist with them and help with your intentions. Let get started!

Herb List

Allspice

This herb is great for bringing in luck, for healing, and money. So if you have a citrine and pretty much any green stone, mineral, or crystal such as green aventurine or green quartz, put that in a little pouch and carry it with you in your pocket or purse. These combinations can help attract money and luck as well.

Aloe

Most of us know that Aloe is a plant that can help treat burns and rashes by putting the Aloe fluid on the area that needs to be treated. Aloe is also great for protection and bringing in luck. When using it for protection, you can simply have it outside your front and back doors with the intention that it will protect you from evil influences and negative energies. You can also cut the leaves and hang them by or above your doors. For me I like to pair Aloe with smokey quartz or black tourmaline. I simply put it in the plant and have it outside my doors. These together were set with the intention that they will protect my house from any evil entity and anything that is not of my God. They guard my house and only allow positive and loving energies inside. Aloe can also bring luck so you can also pair Aloe with citrines and/or golden tiger eye.

Apple

Apple can help bring in love and the ability to heal. If you are doing distant healing for someone, you can simply cut the apple, put the person's name on a piece of paper and put it in the center of the cut apple. Then put the stones that relate to the problem with that person, on it as well. If it is breast cancer, try rhodonite or rose quartz and mend them all together using a string or ribbon and bury it in soil. This will help that person feel so much loving energy, calm, and positive energies. It is best to do this during the waning moon as the moon amplifies the intentions. Please note that these ideas are not to take the place of any doctor's instructions to that person or you. Always remember that the stones abilities and the herbs abilities are only to assist in the healing process.

You can also just insert apple seeds into a crystal grid in any way you like to help with the healing.

As for love, you can put the seeds in a red or pink pouch which also includes crystals for attracting love like, a rose quartz heart, clear quartz heart to amplify, and then emerald to help attract love. It can be attracting a certain someone of interest, just someone to show their love towards you, or bring in loving vibes to you. You can also simply cut the apple in half and give the other half to your love interest, or if you already have a partner, eat it together. While doing that take that time to light some candles and bring out the garnet crystals so that love is filled in the air. It will enhance the happiness in your relationship.

Bamboo

Bamboo is used for protection, luck, breaking hex's, and is the plant of wishing. I feel that this plant would pair well with black tourmaline and black onyx as they both can help protect you from evil intentions brought on by someone else and sends the intention back to its sender 2 times harder. It also absorbs negativity so these stones should be cleansed everyday whether or not they are paired with bamboo or not. You can also pair bamboo with clear quartz or labradorite, or the both of them. Just put them in the plant and tell them your wishes and ask for luck in areas that you need it in. Great and powerful combination.

Bay

I have lots of Bay leaves in my herb cabinet. Bay is great for enhancing psychic abilities, purification, healing in any way, and providing strength within someone else or yourself. Bay is great at your windows as it helps to protect and purify your home. Pair it with selenite or attach to a selenite wand and go through your home or office to purify the space and get rid of any negative energies. Also pairing bay and selenite together can help with really enhancing psychic abilities. Sleep with it under your pillow with the intention that your spirit guides will give you an answer to something that you are questioning in your life. They can help bring visions into your dreams that answer your question. If you are meditating and focusing on ridding yourself or someone else evil intentions brought to that person, or you ridding yourself of those negative energies, add sandalwood to help deepen the cleanse.

Bodhi

Bodhi helps with fertility, deepens meditations, provides protection, and wisdom. Buddha was said to have sat underneath this tree for 6 years meditating. It is said that the leaves of Bodhi still carry his vibrations today. This is why it is so great at enhancing someone's meditative state. The leaves are also said to help females become more fertile and in return, helping them to conceive a baby. Pair the leaves with the larimar stone and watch your meditative state be more focused and deeper than ever. Put this in the plant and give the intention that your spirit guides will protect your home from anything that is not of the angelic realm.

Chamomile

This herb is said to attract money. It can help to make you feel relaxed and can help you to fall asleep. It also helps to remove any negative intentions that were sent to you. A crystal that can be paired with this herb is amethyst.

Chili Pepper

This herb is a powerful herb to help break any bad vibes, intentions, or hex's, that were sent to you. A crystal to go with this herb is black tourmaline.

Cinnamon

Cinnamon is associated with the third eye as it helps to activate the third eye. Put in green tea before meditation to active your third eye. This herb also helps to attract success, aids in spiritual growth, provides protection from negative energies, and also helps to attract love. The perfect crystal to match for this herb is amethyst!

Dandelion

Dandelion is an herb that helps with connecting to the spirit world, it is great for helping with divination, and helps to manifest wishes. A crystal that can work with this herb is labradorite.

Eucalyptus

This herb is said to help bring protection and aids in all healing such as emotional, physical, and spiritual. A great crystal for this herb is clear quartz.

Fig

Fig is an herb that can help with divination, love and fertility. Great crystals for fig is rose quartz or moonstone.

Jasmine

Jasmine helps to bring love, money, and prophetic dreams. A great crystal for this herb would be labradorite.

Juniper

Juniper is a great herb to bring protection from negative energies and evil entities. This is great for exorcisms. This herb is also good for bringing good health. Black tourmaline, black onyx, and smokey quartz are great crystals for this herb. Pretty much the black or brown crystals would be good for this herb.

So as you can see, herbs can play a huge part in amplifying your intentions that you give your crystals or minerals, or even grids. Sprinkle herbs on your grid and give them intentions as well! You can place herbs like lavender in a little pouch with a crystal like, blue lace agate, rose quartz, and amethyst to help you to feel very calm and relaxed so that you can fall asleep and stay asleep! That was just one example of how you can use herbs with crystals. They are even great for meditations and opening up certain chakra points. So try it and see how you like it.

Using Incense and Oils

INCENSE AND OILS I FEEL are important when working with crystals and your intentions because it is a great way of amplifying the energies and your intentions. The smoke from the incense helps to give you a visualization as it helps you to imagine that your intentions are within the smoke and rising above and into the universe! When I think of incense, I think of the smoke as the messenger, sending out your intentions, energies, and vibrations. I see the intentions in words but in smoke form, flowing off into the universe and your surroundings, helping the energies go outward. Same thing with the oils except I visualize the scent going and spreading outward into the universe. So, as you can see, it is simple to add in the oils and incense in with your crystals. You could even make a very pretty grid with your incense and oils. Please note that you must use only a dab of oil on all your crystals because too much oil can damage them.

List of Some Incense

Dragon's Blood- Protects against negative entities, energies, and intentions. It also attracts love.

Frankincense- Protects against negative entities, energies, and intentions. Brings good luck, enhances psychic abilities, and cleanses spaces to help make them pure.

Hibiscus- Great for attracting love.

Jasmine- Helps to bring financial luck and bring prophetic dreams.

Lavender- Helps to relax mind, body, and soul. Great to help you become sleepy when having trouble sleeping at night. Great at attracting love and meditations.

Patchouli- Attracts love, money, and fertility.

Rose- Brings prophetic dreams and helps to attract love to you and spread loving energies out.

Rosemary- Helps to purify people and spaces, rids of nightmares, and aids in personal spiritual healing.

Sandalwood- Exorcises demons and evil entities. Spirits. Great in cleansing and purifying spaces and people. Helps to send off wishes into the universe.

There are many kinds of incense, but these are the ones that most people are familiar with. Once you know what the incense abilities are, you can match the right crystal with them. That is something you now know how to do.

List of Some Oils

Eucalyptus- Healing and purification.

Ginger- Helps you to feel energized, sexually energizes yourself or someone else, and helps to attract love and money.

Lavender- Helps one to feel calm and relaxed.

Lemongrass- Helps to cleanse and purify spaces and people. Also helps to bring psychic awareness.

Lotus- Expands your spirituality, aids in spiritual healing, and enhances meditative state.

Mugwort- Brings psychic awareness, psychic dreams, and aids in astral projection.

Rose- Helps to attract love and spread loving energies.

There are many other oils out there that you can find and use with or even without crystals. Remember that using both oils and crystals will help to amplify the energies and vibrations when used together. Great combination!

7

Candles

CANDLES AND CRYSTALS WORK WONDERFULLY together as the vibrations and energies of the fire help to enhance your intentions. Using a specific color of candle can help also. For example, green is associated with money so burning a green candle with the intention that you will find financial luck, makes sense. In this chapter, I am going to be listing the colors and what they are associated with, and as well as crystals that can be paired with them. Feel free to even pair the crystal and candle with an herb!

Candle Colors and Their Meanings

White

- Goddess or your inner goddess.

- Feminine Energy

- Higher self

- Purity

- Peace

- Use as substitute for any other color

- Moon Stone, Clear Quartz, or others of the same energies

Black

- Protection

- Rids of any negative energies or intentions

- Root Chakra as it help to balance and ground you. Can be red, black, or brown colors.

- Black Onyx, Black Tourmaline, Black Obsidian, or others of the same energies

Brown

- Influences friendship or partnerships

- Helps with bindings

- Jasper crystals or Agate crystals, Turquoise, or others of the same energy

Silver

- Astral projection
- Feminine energies
- Telepathy
- Clairvoyance
- Prophetic dreams
- Intuition
- Labradorite, Angelite, Amethyst, or other crystals of the same energy

Blue

- Element of water
- Wisdom
- Protection
- Throat Chakra
- Brings calming energies
- Angelic and spiritual inspiration
- Communication to higher realms, Angles, and spirit guides
- Celestite, Selenite, Angelite, Amethyst, or other crystals of the same energy

Purple

- Third Eye Chakra
- Enhances psychic abilities

- Brings forth feelings and knowledge that may be hidden from you or hard for you to show.

- Calm and relaxation

- Spiritual power

- Amethyst, Celestite, Aquamarine, Hematite, or other crystals of the same energy

Pink

- Caring

- Romance

- Nurturing

- Affection

- Heart Chakra

- Rose Quartz, Emerald, Pink Tourmaline, Garnet, Peridot, or other crystals of the same energy

Green

- Element of Earth

- Center Chakra

- Success

- Luck

- Money

- Plant and Flower Health

- Growth
- Green Aventurine, Citrine, Moss Agate, Green Tourmaline, Red Jasper, Carnelian, or other crystals of the same energy

Orange

- Success
- Energizes
- Sacral Chakra
- Aids to help conceive
- Carnelian, Citrine, Orange Calcite, Amber, or other crystals of the same energy

Yellow

- Solar Plexus Chakra
- Sun Energy
- Memory
- Mental focus
- Amber, Sun Stone, Citrine, Green Calcite, Emerald, Carnelian, Pyrite, or other crystals of the same energy

Gold

- God
- Happiness

- Masculine Energy

- Sun Stone, Tourmaline family, and other crystals of the same energy

Copper

- Money

- Success within a business

- Growth Professionally

- Aiding in achieving Business/ Money Goals

- Agate family, Pink and Orange Calcite, Citrine, or other crystals that have the same energy

Tarot Cards and Crystals

Tarot cards are something that people tend to be drawn to all the time. The cards are pretty, they look ancient and unique. But, tarot cards are more than just pretty stack of cards with cool pictures, it is a type of divination. Tarot cards are a way of revealing hints to, the present, past, future, and the unknown, to people. It is a system that taps into your higher energies; negative and positive, in order to get the answers. You also tap into contact with your spirit guides, if you wish to. This is in terms of the way you are shifting your life. The tarot can reveal to you what you are doing wrong and the best path to take instead, so that you can correct yourself and your patters in your life.

Now, anyone can own a set of tarot cards, however, not everyone can read them! It takes real practice and study to master these cards and their different layouts! It also takes real concentration and asking your higher self and/or spirit guides to come forth and help to send a message to someone or yourself.

Using crystals with tarot readings is a great idea as it helps to amplify the energies from that person asking the question and implementing them into the cards. The crystals help to draw in the correct energies to the question. This can enhance your chances of getting a clear answer back, which are influenced by the spirit, angels, and spirit guides.

If you are not sure how to begin with Tarot cards, I suggest buying a beginner's kit and practice as much as you can so that you are able to do it without help. Once you feel comfortable then you may add the crystals into your readings. It is important to know that, before using your cards, it is wise to start with an open prayer to protect yourself from any unwanted entities from freely coming through. Prayer creates this Godly protective circle around you as you use your cards. When you are done with your readings, it is best to also perform a closing prayer as well so that you close that portal and connection to source or God (whomever you see as your source).

How do you know what crystals to use? I am sure you are wondering! There are a couple easy ways you can do this. You can go the safe route and just use clear quartz crystals to surround the cards and at least three protectant crystals to place around the cards as well, or you can use a pendulum (next chapter). Lay out a few crystals, then with your pendulum go over each crystal and ask your pendulum, "Should I use this crystal in my reading today?" and wait for your yes or no answer. The next chapter explains how the pendulum works.

Working with a Pendulum

To BEGIN THIS CHAPTER I first want to mention that you go about buying a pendulum based on how much you are attracted to it and how much it draws you in. Not that it looks pretty but how it just draws you in. That would be a way to begin buying a pendulum because sometimes the pendulum crystal may not work well with your energies if you just buy one because it looks cool. Go with your gut and intuition on this purchase. Take your time, relax, breath and brows the pendulums. Which one stands out the most? When I bought my first pendulum, I just bought one because I just wanted one and thought that a clear quartz would work with me no matter what. I was wrong! It broke on me within that first week and I would get too high of a vibration that I would not be able to be around it. Yes, I cleansed it and charged it and let it sit wrapped up in a room before using it. It still did not mesh well with me. It just was not meant to be with me and it had enough energy already that the tip shattered on me and it was only sitting on a table! I have left it outside in my plants ever since.

When I came to buy my second pendulum, I was walking browsing a metaphysical store and all of a sudden my vibration raised. It was not intense, it was just right and I instantly listened to what my higher self was trying to tell me. I figured I should scan the room like a radar and see where this vibration would rise. I went to the pendulums and the instant my eyes locked on a rose quartz chakra pendulum, my vibration shook me and I knew that pendulum was supposed to come home with me. I love that pendulum and I have it with me all the time and work with it to help me find missing things or to help me when I cannot decide on something and need some clear guidance from my spirit guides. Of course I can always tap into my intuitive psychic and mediumship abilities for that but, that is a whole other book for you to wait for.

Once you have bought your pendulum, please cleans it with one of the following: sage, frankincense, nag champa, or palo santos. Allow it to cleanse for a long while as the pendulums, like all crystals, pick up many energies and intentions from others who have touched it. Crystal pendulum or not, cleanse and charge it! Do not use it right away! Keep cleansing it for at least 2-3 days. Don't cleanse it 2-3 days nonstop! Just cleanse for about an hour each day, then charge under a full moon or just any moon light. You may charge it with sun light (15 minutes max in sun light) or candle light but, the full moon lunar energies are so powerful that it is suggested to charge under a full moon.

Once you have completed the cleansing and charging process, place the pendulum away for about a week. I know you want to use it right away!! But you have to let it rest as it is a powerful tool that if too full with energy, it needs a good rest before use. Place it in a cloth and store it away in a sacred space or any space that you feel is a good sacred place for it to "sleep". Once the week has gone by, you then have to spend time with it. Place it in your bra ladies! Allow it to get to know you. You may place it in your pocket as well or just hang out with it while you are watching TV. Just make sure that it is in its cloth and is on you. I recommend sleeping with it as well. Place it in your pillow case. Once you have done that for a week or two, it is ready to activate and use!

Step 1:

Hold the pendulum from the tip of the string and place your other hand below the pendulum point, not touching it. Breath, relax, and come to a calm state. Clear you mind and ask the pendulum to send you its sign for "yes". Please write down what means "yes" and thank your higher self and the pendulum for showing you.

Step 2:

Pick up the pendulum again and this time ask the pendulum to show you its sign for "no". Write down its sign for "no" and thank your higher self and the pendulum for showing you

Step 3:

Pick up the pendulum again and ask it to show you its sign for "You are not ready to know". Write down what means "You are not ready to know" and thank your higher self and the pendulum for showing you.

Once you have gotten the basics down, you are ready to use your pendulum. Please know these are not the only signs that a pendulum can tell you, but because this is a beginner's book, it is best to start off small and then once you get good, work yourself up to more enhanced knowledge. The other knowledge I talk about is like, having your pendulum tell you what chakra points are closed and which ones are open and working for you, just for example. Perhaps I'll write another book going further into all these chapters.

A Quick Letter

THANK YOU FOR READING, "THE Mystical World of Healing Crystals: A Metaphysical Guide". I wrote this little letter just to help clear up a few things about healing crystals and their different uses with other spiritual tools. I know that a lot of people are afraid to expand their spirituality because they are afraid that the ways they want to expand, such as the ways in this book, they feel it might be "bad". Do not fear this. These uses talked about in my book are a way of tapping into your higher self and divine source (your soul and spirit) to gain more insight on life and tapping into communication with your spirit guides so that you have an easier way of communicating with them and asking them for help and guidance. Although no matter where you are, they can hear you and help however, some of us feel a need and draw to communicating with them in this spiritual and fascinating way!

When it comes to using crystals to help with personal, emotional, spiritual, or physical issues or ailments, please note that this does not mean that you should stop taking anything prescribed to you by your doctor! These ways of healing are only meant to aid in the recovery.

I hope that you enjoyed this book and I look forward to providing you with more information in the future!

Crystal Blessings,

Jennifer J Barlow

Bibliography

Moon, H. (2015). Science of Crystal Healing [blog post]. Retrieved from http://hibiscusmooncrystalacademy. com/science-crystal-healing/

Lebron, L. (Year). Healing Crystals [Video file]. Retrieved from YouTube website: https://www.youtube. com/channel/UCTPrjR-PaxwOqX-9dqslMXw

Mideaker, T. (Year). Healing Crystals [Video file]. Retrieved from YouTube website: https://www. youtube.com/channel/UCTPrjR-PaxwOqX-9dqslMXw

Printed in the United States
By Bookmasters